Great Heroes

Henry Billings

Melissa Stone

STECK-VAUGHN
C O M P A N Y
A subsidiary of National Education Corporation

D1444921

Books in this series:

Great Adventures
Great Challenges
Great Firsts
Great Heroes

Acknowledgments

Supervising Editor

Diane Sharpe

Project Editor

Teresa Turner

Designer

Sharon Golden

Photo Editor

Margie Matejcik

Electronic Production

Alan Klemp

Cover Illustration

Terrell Powell

Illustration Credits

Gary McElhaney

Photo Credits

P. 2 Culver Pictures; p. 4 Culver Pictures; p. 5 The Granger Collection, New York; p. 7 Culver Pictures; p. 10 Culver Pictures; p. 11 Culver Pictures; p. 12 The Granger Collection, New York; p. 13 The Bettmann Archive; p. 22 The Bettmann Archive; p. 24 Illinois State Historical Library; p. 25 Culver Pictures; p. 26 The Bettmann Archive; p. 30 Smithsonian Institution; p. 33 Culver Pictures; p. 34 Culver Pictures; p. 35 Culver Pictures; p.46 © Topham/The Image Works; p. 47 © Topham/The Image Works; p. 49 AP/Wide World; p. 52 AP/Wide World; p.53 AP/Wide World; p. 55 AP/Wide World; p. 58 AP/Wide World; p. 61 The Bettmann Archive; p. 63 The Bettmann Archive; p. 66 AP/Wide World; p. 68 AP/Wide World; p. 70 © Charles Moore/Black Star; p. 71 AP/Wide World; p. 74 International Tennis Hall of Fame; p. 75 AP/Wide World; p. 77 AP/Wide World; p. 80 AP/Wide World; p. 81 UPI/Bettmann Newsphotos; p. 83 AP/Wide World

ISBN 0-8114-4691-3

1 2 3 4 5 6 7 8 9 0 PO 95 94 93 92 91 90

Contents

Joan of Arc

Sept. '91

Charles VII of France buried his face in his hands.

"All is lost," he whispered to himself. "Soon England will control this whole country." Suddenly a guard knocked on the door. "King Charles," said the guard, "someone is here to see you."

"Who is it?" asked Charles.

"It is a young girl. She says she has come to lead you into battle. She says she can help you beat the English."

Charles looked at the guard **suspiciously**. "Is this some kind of trick?" he asked. "Who is this girl?"

"Her name is Joan of Arc."

The Voice of an Angel

Until 1425, Joan of Arc was an ordinary girl. She lived with her family in a small village in France. Her life was simple. She never learned to read or write. She never traveled more than a few miles from her home. She spent her days working in the garden and looking after the sheep.

In 1425, however, things changed. In the garden one day, Joan thought she heard a voice. Looking up, she saw a bright light. At first Joan was scared. She dropped to her knees in fear. But then a peaceful feeling came over her. She believed she was hearing the voice of an **angel**.

From then on, Joan often heard the angel's voice. She believed she also heard the voices of dead **saints**. These voices told her that she had been chosen for a special job. They said she had been picked to save France from its enemies.

"I know who the enemies are," thought Joan. "They are English soldiers. I have heard my father speak about them. For years England has been at war with France. Now England is winning the war. The English already control most French cities."

The voices told Joan that she was right. They told her to go to Charles VII, King of France. "You must lead his armies into battle," they told her. "We will guide you. Trust in God, and **victory** shall be yours."

At first, Joan was afraid to do this. She was only 15 years old. She had never spoken to a king. She had never been near a sword or a suit of **armor**. How could she possibly become the leader of an army? Yet the voices kept telling her to go. Finally, in 1429, she could wait no longer. She believed she had to act. She believed that it was up to her to save her country.

King Charles VII of France

A Special Sword

When Joan arrived at Charles VII's castle, he thought she might be playing a trick on him. He decided to test her. He gathered 200 men and women in a large hall. He took off his crown and dressed like the other guests. Then he told the guard to bring in Joan.

"If she really has special powers, she should be able to find me even in this crowd," he thought.

When Joan entered the room, she walked directly toward Charles. She moved past everyone else until she came to him. Then she dropped to her knees, saying, "In God's name, you are the true King of France."

Charles was amazed. Clearly, Joan was not playing tricks. He decided to listen to her plan.

Joan told Charles that she would help him save the city of Orleans. This was one of the few French cities which the English did not already control. For six months, English soldiers had been trying to take over Orleans. They had built walls and towers to cut the city off from the rest of France. The people inside the city could not get fresh food or supplies. They were growing hungrier each day. Any day now, they would open their gates and **surrender** to the English.

"We must go to Orleans," Joan said to Charles. "We must beat back the English and free the city." Charles agreed to do as Joan said. He ordered his men to bring her a suit of armor. He had a white flag made for her. He also offered her a beautiful sword. Joan took the armor and the flag. But she did not take the sword.

"There is a church in the village of Fierbois," said Joan. "It is called the Church of St. Catherine. There you will find a sword buried in the ground. It has five crosses on its blade. That is the sword I want."

No one in Fierbois had heard of any sword in the church. "What makes you think there is such a sword?" asked Charles.

"The voice of St. Catherine herself told me," said Joan.

Charles ordered his men to look for the sword. To their surprise, they did find an old sword there. It had been buried for many years. And the sword did have five crosses on its blade. To Charles and his army, this was further proof that Joan had special powers.

Saving Orleans

On April 27, 1429, Joan led Charles and his men toward Orleans. For two days, they marched through enemy land. At last they neared Orleans.

"The rest of my army will meet us here in a few days," Charles told Joan. "Let us rest until they arrive."

Joan of Arc leads the French to victory.

Joan agreed. But on the night of May 4, she suddenly jumped out of bed. The voices had spoken again. They told her to fight, and fight now!

"We must hurry," she told Charles as she put on her armor. "Gather what men you have and follow me." With her flag waving, Joan led the men toward the English soldiers. She showed no fear. Her face glowed with **confidence.** With Joan to lead them, the French soldiers felt new hope. They believed "Joan the Maid" would lead them to victory.

For three days the French fought bravely. Again and again they attacked the English. On the second day, an arrow hit Joan in the shoulder. Still, she kept fighting. At last, on May 7, 1429, the English turned and ran away from Orleans. The French soldiers cheered.

Joan of Arc had saved the city of Orleans. More than that, she had made the French believe in themselves again. She had shown them that they could win the war.

From that moment on, Joan of Arc was their hero. For the next few months, Joan led the French to victory after victory. In 1430, she was captured by the English and later killed. Even today, her **memory** continues to **inspire** the French people. Her name will forever bring thoughts of hope and **courage**.

Do You Remember?

■ Read each sentence below. Write **T** if the sentence is true. Write **F** if the sentence is false.

_____ 1. France was at war with Russia.

_____ 2. Joan of Arc did not know how to read or write.

_____ 3. Joan's mother was married to the king of France.

_____ 4. Joan believed she heard the voice of an angel.

_____ 5. Joan picked King Charles VII out of a crowd of 200 people.

_____ 6. Joan asked for a sword that was buried in a barn.

_____ 7. Joan led the French army in the battle to save Orleans.

_____ 8. Joan was killed in the battle of Orleans.

Express Yourself

■ Pretend you are Joan of Arc. What would you say to King Charles to make him believe that you should be allowed to lead the French Army against the English?

_____

_____

_____

_____

_____

_____

_____

Exploring Words

■ Use the words in the box to complete the paragraphs. Reread the paragraphs to be sure they make sense.

armor	surrender	memory	courage	confidence
saints	victory	angel	inspire	suspiciously

Joan of Arc was in her garden when she first heard the voice of an (1) _____. Later, Joan also heard the voices of dead (2) _____. These voices told Joan to go to the king of France. They told her to lead the French army against the English. The king of France greeted Joan (3) _____. Soon, however, he agreed to follow her plan. Joan put on a suit of (4) _____. As she led the French army into battle, her face shone with (5) _____. She led her men to (6) _____. Because of her, the town of Orleans did not (7) _____ to the English.

Many battles later, Joan was captured and killed by the English. Still, her (8) _____ lived on. Everyone remembered her (9) _____. Her actions helped to (10) _____ the French people.

9

A Pirate's Last Stand

The people of North Carolina were **terrified**. At night, they locked themselves in their houses. They prayed that their lives and property would be **spared**.

The cause of all this terror was one man — the **pirate** Blackbeard. No one dared to stand up to him. But among themselves, the people whispered, "Something must be done. We can't keep living like this. Blackbeard takes whatever he wants from us. Soon we will all be ruined."

Terror of the Seas

Blackbeard was known the world over for his long, black beard. This beard covered his whole face. Blackbeard braided his beard and tied the ends with ribbons. Then he wrapped the braids around his ears. He was a huge man with wild eyes.

Throughout 1717 and 1718, Blackbeard sailed the waters off the Carolina coast. He traveled in a ship called Queen Anne's Revenge. Blackbeard would capture ships and steal their cargo. Then he would kill the sailors or leave them to die on small islands.

Sometimes Blackbeard left the sea and attacked North Carolina towns. He and his band of pirates robbed many homes. They would kill anyone who tried to stop them. The people of North Carolina asked their **governor**, Charles Eden, to protect them. But Governor Eden had become friends with the pirate. Blackbeard gave Eden money. In return, Eden promised to leave Blackbeard alone.

Pirates force a man to walk the plank.

At last the people of North Carolina could stand it no longer. They went to Governor Spotswood of Virginia. Spotswood agreed that Blackbeard had to be stopped. "I will send the Navy out after him," he said.

There was one man in the Navy who was not afraid of Blackbeard. That man was a brave young **lieutenant** named Robert Maynard. Governor Spotswood asked Maynard to lead a group of men against the pirate.

"Shall I take him dead or alive?" asked Maynard.

"I don't care," said Spotswood. "Just get rid of him."

In Search of Blackbeard

Maynard and his crew set out at once in search of Blackbeard. On November 17, 1718, he discovered Blackbeard's hiding place, Ocracoke Inlet.

Maynard gathered his men together. "In the morning," he said, "we'll sail up the inlet and attack Blackbeard."

One of Maynard's men spoke up. "Lieutenant, the Queen Anne's Revenge has many cannons. We have no cannons. How can we hope to beat Blackbeard?"

"We will have to make a surprise attack," answered Maynard.

On November 22, Maynard and his men rowed toward the Queen Anne's Revenge. Suddenly a shot was fired from the pirate ship. Maynard raised his flag, and continued toward the ship. When Maynard and his men were close enough, Blackbeard **demanded** to know who they were.

"You see by our **colors** we are no pirates," answered Maynard.

Maynard's answer made Blackbeard angry. He warned Maynard and his men that he would give no **quarter**.

Maynard showed no fear. "I do not expect quarter from you, nor shall I give any," he said.

Face to Face

The <u>Queen Anne's Revenge</u> was stuck in the sand. If Maynard and his men were quick enough, they could attack the ship from the front. There were no cannons there. But once the **tide** came in, the pirate ship could turn its cannons to face the boats.

Maynard's men weren't fast enough. The pirates got free of the sand and fired at them. Many men were killed. Still Maynard didn't give up. He had an idea. He ordered all the men to go below except himself and the man steering. Then they sailed up close to the pirate ship.

When Blackbeard saw the empty ship, he laughed. "Come on," he said to his men. "Let's go finish them off!" With that, Blackbeard and some of his pirates jumped onto Maynard's ship. At once, the rest of Maynard's men came up from below and attacked the pirates.

Blackbeard and Maynard saw each other across the deck. They worked their way toward one another. At last, they were face to face. The two men fired their guns at the same time. Blackbeard missed. Maynard's bullet hit the pirate. But Blackbeard did not fall.

Through the smoke, Blackbeard leaped at Maynard with his sword waving. With one blow, he cut the blade off Maynard's sword. Blackbeard raised his sword to strike again. Maynard's men wounded the pirate with their swords. Still he didn't fall. They shot at him with their guns. Finally Blackbeard fell to the deck, dead. The few pirates who were left alive gave themselves up.

"At last!" said Maynard. "The people of North Carolina can again live in peace."

People all along the coast celebrated. Sailors everywhere **rejoiced.** Lieutenant Robert Maynard had put an end to one of the cruelest pirates ever to sail the seas.

Do You Remember?

■ In the blank, write the letter of the best ending for each sentence.

_____ 1. Blackbeard was a pirate who
    a. built ships.
    b. captured ships and stole their cargo.
    c. gave money to the poor.

_____ 2. Blackbeard was known the world over for
    a. his long, black beard   b. being kind   c. his good looks.

_____ 3. Governor Spotswood asked Robert Maynard to
    a. get rid of Blackbeard.
    b. help Blackbeard.
    c. talk Blackbeard into leaving.

_____ 4. Maynard hated
    a. Governor Spotswood.   b. Queen Anne.   c. pirates.

_____ 5. The Queen Anne's Revenge was hidden in
    a. a cave.   b. Ocracoke Inlet.   c. a forest.

_____ 6. Maynard and his men had no
    a. swords.   b. cannons.   c. food.

_____ 7. After Blackbeard fell, the pirates who were left alive
    a. kept fighting.   b. swam away.   c. gave themselves up.

Critical Thinking – Finding the Sequence

■ Write **1** before the sentence that tells what happened first in the story. Write **2** before the sentence that tells what happened next, and so on.

_____ Maynard and his crew found Blackbeard's hiding place.

_____ Sailors everywhere rejoiced.

_____ The people asked Governor Spotswood to help them.

_____ Governor Spotswood asked Maynard to get rid of Blackbeard.

_____ Blackbeard jumped onto Maynard's ship.

14

Exploring Words

■ Write the correct word in each sentence.

terrified	spared	pirate	governor	lieutenant
demanded	colors	quarter	tide	rejoiced

1. A sailor who robs other ships is a _____.

2. Something that has not been harmed has been _____.

3. If you _____, you felt glad about something.

4. A _____ is an officer in the Army or Navy.

5. To be very frightened is to be _____.

6. A _____ is the leader in charge of a state.

7. The rising and falling of the oceans is the _____.

8. If you asked for something as though it was your right,

   you _____ it.

9. If you are kind to your enemies and do not kill them, you give them

   _____.

10. A flag that shows who you are is called your _____.

Fighting for Freedom

Bernardo O'Higgins held his mother's hands. He said softly, "I think we should leave Chile. José Carrera and his family are ruining this country. They are terrible rulers. They don't care at all about the Chilean people. We have friends in Argentina. Maybe things would be better there."

Just then there was a knock on the door. A neighbor brought bad news. Soldiers from Peru had just **invaded** Chile. Once again, Chile was in danger of falling under Spanish rule. "I have changed my mind," said O'Higgins angrily. "This is no time to leave. We must stay and fight!"

The Battle of Rancagua

The people of Chile wanted to rule themselves. In 1810, they had taken their first step. They had gotten rid of the Spanish governor. By 1811, they had set up their own government.

But things did not run smoothly. The new leaders fought among themselves. Peruvian leaders, who were **loyal** to Spain, saw their chance to bring Spanish rule back to Chile. On March 27, 1813, the leader of Peru ordered his soldiers to move against Chile. When the Peruvian soldiers arrived in Chile, O'Higgins decided right away that he would stay to fight them. To save his country, he even agreed to serve under Carrera. O'Higgins took command of a small army.

Although he was not trained as a soldier, O'Higgins was a brave leader. In one battle, he was shot in the leg. He bandaged the leg himself. He then told his men to carry him back to the fighting. His courage lifted the spirits of the Chilean soldiers.

Carrera, however, was not a good leader. His army lost most of the battles it fought. The final blow came in October, 1814, in the town of Rancagua. The battle lasted for two days. Each side raised a black flag. That meant they would fight to the death. It was the **bloodiest** battle in the history of Chile. O'Higgins and about 200 soldiers managed to fight their way out of town. From a safe distance, O'Higgins turned and looked at the smoke rising over the town. "The war is lost. **Foreigners** control our country once again," he said sadly to his men.

Planning His Return

O'Higgins then **fled** from Chile. He and some of his soldiers crossed the Andes Mountains into Argentina. O'Higgins did not want to stay there. He wanted to return to Chile. "But first," he said to himself, "I have to rebuild the army. Then I will defeat the Peruvians and free Chile once and for all."

In Argentina, O'Higgins met José de San Martín. Like O'Higgins, San Martín was a great freedom fighter. He wanted to drive the Spanish out of Chile and the rest of South America. One way to do that, he decided, was to help O'Higgins.

It took over two years to get ready. But by the end of 1816, San Martín and O'Higgins had an army. They called it the Army of the Andes. It was made up of 4,000 soldiers. The people of Argentina helped this army greatly. The women sewed **uniforms**. Church leaders sent church bells to be melted down for cannons and swords. Local farmers gave up their oxen and mules to help move supplies. Finally, on January 18, 1817, the Army of the Andes began its march.

Across the Andes to Victory

San Martín and O'Higgins wanted to strike near Chile's **capital** city. That meant they had to cross the Andes

through a pass called Los Patos. It was over 20,000 feet high. The ground was icy and covered with snow. The men suffered from the cold and from the thin air. Over 5,000 mules and 1,000 horses died. But not a single man died, and not a single rifle was lost.

On February 2, San Martín and O'Higgins looked down at the fields of Chile. The moment had come. Their army caught the Peruvians by surprise. The Peruvians were easily beaten. "We have come to free you from foreign rule," O'Higgins told the cheering Chileans.

On February 12, O'Higgins and his men fought another battle. It took place in the town of Chacbuco. O'Higgins led the attack. The fighting was bloody, but O'Higgins never gave up. Again and again, he charged at the enemy. After thirty minutes, the battle was over. The Peruvians fled in **defeat**. "This is the happiest day of my life," thought O'Higgins.

At last, Chile was free. The Chilean people quickly chose Bernardo O'Higgins to be their new leader. "In the space of 24 days," said San Martín, "we have crossed the highest mountain range in the world, overthrown the **tyrants**, and given **liberty** to Chile."

Do You Remember?

■ Read each sentence below. Write **T** if the sentence is true. Write **F** if the sentence is false.

_____ 1. Bernardo O'Higgins was a brave leader.

_____ 2. José Carrera was a great leader.

_____ 3. After the battle of Rancagua, O'Higgins and his soldiers fled to Argentina.

_____ 4. José de San Martín refused to help O'Higgins fight for Chile's freedom.

_____ 5. The Army of the Andes was led by José Carrera.

_____ 6. The Army of the Andes crossed mountains that were over 20,000 feet high.

_____ 7. The Peruvians destroyed the Army of the Andes.

_____ 8. O'Higgins was chosen to be the new leader of Chile.

Express Yourself

■ Pretend you are Bernardo O'Higgins. Your Army of the Andes is about to cross the mountains to fight for Chile's freedom. Write a short speech to your soldiers to get them ready for this difficult journey.

_____

_____

_____

_____

_____

_____

Exploring Words

■ Use the clues to complete the puzzle. Choose from the words in the box.

invaded
bloodiest
loyal
foreigners
fled
uniforms
capital
defeat
tyrants
liberty

Across

1. true to something
4. causing the greatest harm to many people
6. cruel leaders
7. entered by force
9. clothing that soldiers wear

Down

1. freedom
2. ran away from
3. people from another country
5. the seat of a government
8. the act of losing

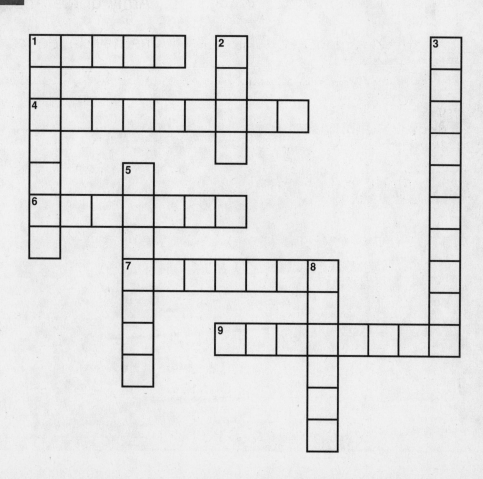

Voice for the Children

Florence Kelley stared in **horror** at the giant room full of furnaces. "So this is what a glass factory is like," she thought. The only light in the room came from the flaming furnaces. In front of these furnaces, glass blowers sat working. At the same time, dozens of young boys hurried around the room. Some carried heavy buckets of water for the blowers. Others sat next to the furnaces, cleaning tools. The boys looked tired and dirty. They had cuts and burns on their hands from the hot glass.

"I can't believe it!" Florence thought angrily. "I can't believe young boys work in places like this!"

Florence Kelly

Dirt, Disease, and Danger

Florence Kelley was only twelve years old when she visited this Pennsylvania glass factory. Her father took her there late one night in 1871. He wanted to show her the wonders of America's new factories. He wanted her to see how quickly things could be made. Kelley did see this. But she also saw how awful the factory was for child workers. The image of small boys **crouching** by the hot furnaces never left her. "It was a picture I carried with me all my days," she later wrote.

As Kelley grew older, she learned that these boys were not alone. In 1880, over one million children worked in hot, crowded, unsafe factories. Often they worked twelve hours a day, six or seven days a week. They worked making cloth, glass, books, baskets, candy, and more. Almost all factory owners **hired** children. They did it to save money. They didn't have to pay children as much as older workers.

"But children should be in school!" Kelley cried. "They should not be doing such dangerous work!"

The work was indeed dangerous. Every year tens of thousands of child workers were hurt or killed. In some factories, children handled pots of **acid** or boiling water. Often these children ended up with bad burns. In other factories, children ran large machines. Some of these children lost fingers, arms, or legs while trying to do their jobs.

In most factories, the workers had no fresh air. Children had no protection from the dirt and **disease** of the factories. Finally, many factory owners kept their workroom doors locked. When a fire broke out, the workers inside could not escape. Many child workers lost their lives in factory fires.

Leading the Fight

"Something must be done!" said Kelley. In 1889, she wrote a paper called "Our **Toiling** Children." She told of the horrors children faced in factories. She asked all Americans to help change things. "Do not buy goods that were made by child workers!" she cried. "Buy goods from companies that don't hire children!"

Kelley also asked the government to step in. She wanted new laws that would keep children out of factories. She wanted a law forcing all children under 16 years of age to stay in school.

Kelley worked hard to earn support for her ideas. She gave speeches and wrote reports. She spoke to anyone who would listen. Within a few years, she had become famous. Everyone knew her as a leader in the fight against child **labor**.

In 1893, Florence Kelley fought for a new law in Illinois. It was designed to improve factories. The law said factory owners could not hire young children. Only people fourteen years old and older could work in factories. The law also created a Chief Factory **Inspector** for the state. This person would make sure factories were following the new law.

Kelley was delighted when the law was passed. "At last changes are being made!" she said. One month later, she was even more excited. The Governor of Illinois asked her to be the Chief Factory Inspector.

A Job Well Done

Kelley's first months as Inspector were not easy. Day after day she traveled to dark, dirty factories. She ordered the factory owners to stop using young workers.

"I won't do that!" shouted one owner angrily.

"Very well," said Kelley. "Then I shall take you to court." In fact, Kelley did take several owners to court. She forced them to pay fines for breaking the law.

Before long, owners hated to see Kelley coming. Many were **rude** to her. Some made **threats**. One went even further. As Kelley approached his factory, he took out his gun. He fired a couple of warning shots at her.

"That ought to scare her off," he muttered. But he was wrong. Although Kelley's life was in danger, she would not stop her work. She cared more about the safety of children than she did about her own safety.

In her second year as Inspector, Kelley faced a new problem. Smallpox broke out in Illinois. Many people died of it. Kelley knew that smallpox was easily passed from one person to another. It could even be passed along in clothing. The best way to stop smallpox was to keep the sick people away from everyone else. Any clothing made by sick people should also be kept away.

"That is not happening," Kelley thought. "Sick people are still sewing clothes. They are passing the disease on to all the child workers. And the damage doesn't stop there. The clothes they make are sold in stores. When people buy these clothes, they carry smallpox home with them."

Kelley knew she had to act. She visited workroom after workroom. Whenever she found sick workers, she made them stop working. She also found a way to get rid of the clothes they had made.

"Burn them!" she ordered owners. "Burn all the clothes made by your sick workers."

"That will cost thousands of dollars!" screamed one owner.

"I know," said Kelley. "But burn them anyway."

Factory owners were very angry. Still, Kelley did not back down. Under her direction, thousands of dollars worth of clothing were burned.

When Florence Kelley's time as Inspector was over, there was still much to be done. Many factories were still unsafe. Many owners still forced workers to work long hours. And some owners were still trying to use child workers. Yet Kelley had started to change the way people think. In Illinois and across the country, people were starting to see that it was wrong to use child workers. Florence Kelley never gave up the fight to protect America's children.

Do You Remember?

■ In the blank, write the letter of the best ending for each sentence.

_____ 1. When Florence Kelley was twelve years old, she saw boys working in a
a. circus.   b. school.   c. factory.

_____ 2. Kelley thought children should
a. go to church.   b. be in school.   c. work part time.

_____ 3. One factory owner tried to scare Kelley away with a
a. gun.   b. dog.   c. car.

_____ 4. Smallpox could be carried by
a. books.   b. clothing.   c. glass.

_____ 5. Kelley made factory owners burn thousands of dollars worth of
a. hay.   b. food.   c. clothes.

Critical Thinking – Drawing Conclusions

■ Finish each sentence by writing the best answer.

1. Many child workers lost their lives in factory fires because _____

_____

2. Kelley wrote "Our Toiling Children" because _____

_____

3. Factory owners hated to see Kelley coming because _____

_____

4. Kelley made factory owners burn clothes made by sick workers

because _____

_____

Exploring Words

■ Find the best meaning for the word in dark print. Fill in the circle next to it.

1. Florence Kelley felt **horror** when she saw the glass factory.
   ○ a. fear and dislike   ○ b. joy   ○ c. cold

2. Kelley saw small boys **crouching** by the hot furnaces.
   ○ a. sleeping   ○ b. bending down   ○ c. eating

3. Most factory owners in America **hired** children
   ○ a. fed   ○ b. turned away   ○ c. gave jobs to

4. Some children handled pots of **acid**.
   ○ a. a chemical that can burn you   ○ b. soup   ○ c. water

5. Children who worked in factories had no protection against **disease**.
   ○ a. hunger
   ○ b. something that makes you sick
   ○ c. being fired

6. Florence Kelley wrote a paper called "Our **Toiling** Children."
   ○ a. curving   ○ b. following   ○ c. working hard

7. Kelley became the Chief Factory **Inspector** for Illinois.
   ○ a. a person who makes sure rules are being followed
   ○ b. a new worker
   ○ c. a machine that makes things smaller

8. Kelley worked against child **labor**.
   ○ a. schooling   ○ b. rights   ○ c. work

9. Some factory workers were **rude** to Kelley.
   ○ a. ready to help   ○ b. kind   ○ c. not polite

10. Some factory owners made **threats** against Kelley.
    ○ a. TV ads   ○ b. promises to do harm   ○ c. promises to help

Chief Joseph

hief Joseph spoke quietly. "We are an **honorable** people," he said. "We have always been friendly to white **settlers**. We have never killed a white person, and we have never broken our promise."

The white leaders nodded. They knew this was true. The Nez Percés had been good friends. They had **welcomed** settlers without anger or fear.

Joseph continued. "I ask you, then, not to drive us off our land. This is where our fathers and mothers are buried. We do not ask much. We only ask that you let us stay on the land we love."

The Beginnings of War

The whites did not do as Joseph asked. They wanted all the good land for themselves. They didn't care about the Native Americans. In 1877, they gave Joseph an order. "You and the other chiefs must move your people out of Oregon's Wallowa Valley. Take them to a reservation. We will give you thirty days. If you have not moved by then, we will use force." Joseph was very upset. He called the Nez Percé chiefs together and told them the news.

"We will not move!" cried Joseph's younger brother, Ollikut. "We will stay and fight!" Several of the other chiefs echoed these words.

Joseph stood up. He knew they couldn't win a war against the Army. "It is better to live at peace than to begin a war and lie dead," he reminded the chiefs. After a long talk, they agreed. They decided to move out of the valley. They told their people to begin packing. They gathered as many of their animals as they could. Then they headed toward the reservation.

On June 13, 1877, the Nez Percés **neared** the reservation. But suddenly three of the younger warriors slipped away. They were bursting with anger over the way the whites had **treated** them. These warriors charged through a **settlement** and killed eighteen people. They got other Nez Percés to join them in a war against the whites. Joseph tried to talk his people out of it, but they would not listen. And so finally, Joseph agreed to fight also. "I will not desert my people," he told Ollikut. "If they are going to fight, I will fight with them."

Running for Safety

The Nez Percés hid in the mountains and canyons of Idaho. Then the chiefs met to make their plans. Several of the chiefs were great warriors. Ollikut was one. Looking

Glass, Five Wounds, and Rainbow were others. Joseph had never been a warrior, but he was a strong leader in another way. His courage and honor inspired people. He had the important job of protecting the women, children, and old people.

Within days, the Army came after the Nez Percés. Again and again the Army attacked. But the Nez Percés knew the land. They knew how to hide in canyons. They knew how to follow streams and climb mountains. Each time the Army attacked, the Nez Percés escaped. In early July, the Nez Percé chiefs held another meeting. "We must decide what to do," said Joseph. "So far we have escaped the Army, but at great cost. Our warriors are tired. Some are dead. Our women and children are frightened and hungry. We cannot keep up the fighting. We must have another plan."

Looking Glass spoke up. He said, "The whites will not let us live in the Wallowa Valley. But that does not mean we must go to a reservation. I believe we should go to a new land where we can live in peace. I believe we should join the Crow tribe to our east."

Chief Joseph

"They live on the other side of the Bitterroot Mountains," said Ollikut. "That is many miles from here. The journey would be long and very difficult."

"It will be a hard journey," said Joseph. "But I think Looking Glass is right. I believe we should join the Crow. Surely the whites will not bother us there." On July 16, the Nez Percés headed toward Montana, the land of the Crow. They crossed the mountains and headed down into the valleys. As they traveled, they passed through several white settlements. "Do not bother the settlers," Joseph ordered. "Leave them alone." The Nez Percés followed Joseph's order. They passed peacefully through all the settlements.

When the Nez Percés reached Big Hole Valley, they stopped to rest. Ollikut turned to Joseph with a smile. He said, "I think at last we are safe." Joseph smiled back. That night he sat quietly with his wife and baby daughter. He felt hopeful that his people would find happiness here on the Montana plains.

That hope did not last long. Early in the morning of August 9, the Army attacked again. The attack took the Nez Percés by surprise. Many were killed in their beds. Others were badly **injured**. Joseph's wife was among those hurt. Joseph scooped up his baby daughter. Holding her in one arm, he bravely fought off the whites. Then he and the other warriors hurried for the safety of the woods.

That night, the Nez Percés held a secret meeting. "At last we know the truth," Joseph said sadly. "We will never be safe in this country. We must keep running until we reach Canada."

The other chiefs agreed. Clearly the Army would not rest until they had wiped out the Nez Percés or put them on a reservation. The tribe's only hope now was to get to Canada.

The End of the Trail

Quickly the Nez Percés moved toward the east. They cleared the last of the Bitterroot Mountains and turned north. They covered hundreds of miles. With each step, Joseph **urged** them to go faster. He knew the Army was not far behind. Twice the Army caught up with them. Both times the Nez Percés fought the soldiers off.

Finally the Nez Percés stopped. Perhaps they were simply too tired to go any further. Perhaps they thought the Army had stopped chasing them. Or perhaps they thought they were already in Canada. Whatever the reason, they set up camp 30 miles south of Canada. There, on September 30, the Army found them.

Again the fighting was bloody. This time the Nez Percés did not have much strength left. They were cold and tired. Many were starving. On October 5, Joseph called together the chiefs who were still alive.

"We must surrender," Joseph said softly. "For the sake of our women and children, we must give up."

Later that morning, Joseph surrendered to General O. O. Howard. "I am tired of fighting," he said. "Our chiefs are killed. It is cold and we have no blankets. The little children are freezing to **death**. My heart is sick and sad. From where the sun now stands, I will fight no more forever." With that, the brave and **noble** Chief Joseph laid down his rifle.

Do You Remember?

■ Read each sentence below. Write **T** if the sentence is true. Write **F** if the sentence is false.

_____ 1. The Nez Percé chiefs wanted to live on a reservation.

_____ 2. White settlers wanted the Nez Percés to leave the Wallowa Valley.

_____ 3. Looking Glass, Rainbow, and Five Wounds were three of Chief Joseph's horses.

_____ 4. Chief Joseph was a great warrior.

_____ 5. Chief Joseph's wife was injured when the Army attacked.

_____ 6. The Nez Percés decided to go to Canada.

_____ 7. Chief Joseph was killed in a fight with the Army.

_____ 8. Chief Joseph surrendered to the Army.

Express Yourself

■ Pretend you belong to the Nez Percé tribe. Would you have gone to the reservation, or would you have joined your people in a fight against the Army? Why?

_____

_____

_____

_____

_____

_____

_____

Exploring Words

■ Use the words in the box to complete the paragraph. Reread the paragraphs to be sure they make sense.

settlements	treated	injured	death	honorable
welcomed	urged	settlers	noble	neared

The Nez Percés were **(1)** _____ people. They had always

(2) _____ white **(3)** _____ onto their land. Whites,

however, **(4)** _____ the Nez Percés badly. In 1877, the Army

ordered the Nez Percés to move to a reservation. Chief Joseph knew

the Nez Percés couldn't win a war against the Army. He

(5) _____ his people to go to the reservation. But instead,

the Nez Percés decided to fight.

Some Nez Percés were killed. Many more were **(6)** _____

in fighting with the Army. Soon the Nez Percés decided to go to

Montana. On their way, they passed peacefully through several white

(7) _____. When the Army attacked them again, the Nez

Percés headed north. They were caught as they **(8)** _____

Canada. Chief Joseph knew that he had to surrender. His people were

hungry. Some were freezing to **(9)** _____. On October 5, 1877,

the **(10)** _____ Chief Joseph laid down his gun.

Teacher with a Dream

Mrs. Patsy McLeod opened the door to her tiny cabin. "Come on," she called to eight-year-old Mary. "It is time to deliver the wash."

"Yes, Mama," said Mary, running to help her mother. Together she and Mrs. McLeod carried the clean clothes to the house up the road. This house was where the white people lived. Mary, a poor black girl, liked going there. She enjoyed seeing the beautiful things inside. On this day, she picked up a book lying on the table. The daughter of the white owner grabbed it away from her. "Put that down," the girl snapped. "You can't read!"

Learning to Read

It hurt Mary to know that the girl was right. She couldn't read. On the way home, she looked up at her mother. "I want to learn to read," she said.

In 1883, there were no schools for black children in Mayesville, South Carolina. But Mary didn't lose hope. As she picked cotton in the fields, she sang to herself, "I'm going to read, I'm going to read."

Two years later, a black woman named Emma Wilson came to Mayesville. She set up a school for black children. Miss Wilson asked the McLeods if any of their children could **attend**. Mr. McLeod thought of his seventeen children. He knew they would all love to go. But he needed them to help pick cotton on the family farm. He could only spare one worker. He decided Mary should be the one to go. And so, a few days later, Mary walked the five miles to the new school. It was just a small room in a **shack**. But Mary didn't care. At last she was going to learn how to read!

Mary did well at school. Soon she could read the Bible. In the evenings, she taught her brothers and sisters to read. Mary also learned arithmetic. She went to the

market with her father to make sure he wasn't cheated when he sold his cotton. "I made my learning useful every way I could," Mary later said.

Becoming a Teacher

Mary **graduated** from Emma Wilson's school in 1888 at the age of 12. There was no nearby high school for black children. So she went back to the farm. Soon Old Bush, the family mule, died. Mary put on the harness and pulled the plow herself. She later said, "My **soul** sat in darkness. I wondered if I would take the place of Old Bush the rest of my days."

Again, however, help came her way. A woman named Mary Chrissman from Denver, Colorado, wanted to help blacks. She offered to pay to send one black girl to high school. When Emma Wilson found out about this offer, she gave Chrissman Mary's name.

With Chrissman's help, Mary spent seven years at Scotia **Seminary** in Concord, North Carolina. She took high school and college classes. She was an **outstanding** student. She studied hard during the days. At night, she worked washing floors, baking bread, and waiting on tables. On June 13, 1894, she graduated from Scotia. Mary wanted to help others. "Miss Chrissman believed in me," she said to herself. "Now it's my turn to offer hope to others." For the next few years, Mary taught at several different schools. In 1898, she met and married Albertus Bethune.

In 1904, Mary McLeod Bethune moved to Florida. She wanted to open her own school for black children. But how could she do it? She had just $1.50 in her pocket. Mary found an empty shack with seven small rooms. The rent was $11 a month. To raise the money, Mary baked sweet potato pies. She sold these pies to workers in the railroad yards. Soon she had enough money to pay the rent.

Next Mary had to find students. She went to the poor black families of Daytona Beach. She found five girls whose parents could afford to pay 50 cents a week. Mary's own son was the sixth student. Mary had no supplies for her students. But that didn't stop her. She made ink by squeezing juice from berries. She made pencils from burned wood. She used boxes for desks. She turned peach baskets upside down for seats. She even begged for supplies door-to-door. She later said, "Many people gave me things just to get rid of me."

Somehow she managed to open her school on October 3, 1904. Mary was a wonderful teacher. Her students quickly learned to read, write, and count. They helped raise money for the school by singing in churches and hotels.

Word about Mary's school spread quickly. Other families wanted to send their children to Mary's school. Some were too poor to pay the 50 cents a week. Mary took them in anyway. She made them new clothes. She taught them to sew and cook for themselves. Soon even adults wanted to attend Mary's school. So Mary began teaching evening classes. In just two years, the school had four teachers and 250 students.

Making a Dream Come True

Mary needed more room. She wanted to buy land so she wouldn't have to pay rent. But she couldn't afford

good land. She went to the owner of the town garbage **dump** and asked to buy it. "Why on earth do you want this land?" the owner asked.

"I don't see a dump," she answered. "I see thousands of boys and girls walking through open doors." The owner asked for $200. Mary paid $5 right away. She promised to pay the rest over the next two years. Again, she baked sweet potato pies to raise money. Then she and her students went to work. They burned or carted off the garbage. Slowly they cleared the land.

Mary knew that she and her students could not make it on their own. They needed money. Mary called on everyone in town. She could talk almost anyone into helping her. She asked one wealthy business leader to support her school. He agreed, but first asked to see it. When he saw the shack and the peach baskets, he asked, "Where is this school?" "In my mind," Mary answered. "And in my soul."

In 1907, after years of hard work, Mary's dream came true. A new four-story school building stood on the old town dump. She named it **Faith** Hall. Over the door it said, "Enter to Learn." On the other side it said, "**Depart** to Serve." Mary McLeod Bethune lived up to those words. She continued to serve her students and **educate** others about the needs of black Americans until her death in 1955.

Do You Remember?

■ In the blank, write the letter of the best ending for each sentence.

_____ 1. As a young girl, Mary wanted to
        a. become a dancer.   b. learn to read.   c. move to Africa.

_____ 2. Mary raised money for her school by
        a. selling pies.   b. training horses.   c. working in a factory.

_____ 3. Mary was a wonderful
        a. painter.   b. driver.   c. teacher.

_____ 4. Mary held evening classes for
        a. blind people.   b. adults.   c. whites.

_____ 5. To get land for her school, Mary bought
        a. the town dump.   b. a pond.   c. an old train station.

Critical Thinking – Fact or Opinion

■ Write **F** before each statement that is a fact. Write **O** before each statement that is an opinion.

_____ 1. Mary's family was poor.

_____ 2. The girl was right to grab the book away from Mary.

_____ 3. Emma Wilson's school for black children was a good idea.

_____ 4. Mary pulled the plow after Old Bush died.

_____ 5. A woman in Denver paid for Mary to attend Scotia Seminary.

_____ 6. It was foolish of Mary to try to open a school for black children.

_____ 7. Mary taught her students to read, write, and count.

_____ 8. Mary's sweet potato pies were the best ever made.

_____ 9. Mary should not have built her school on the town dump.

_____10. Mary named the new school building Faith Hall.

Exploring Words

■ Write the correct word in each sentence.

attend	shack	graduated	soul	seminary
dump	faith	outstanding	depart	educate

1. A place where people take their garbage is a _____.

2. To teach is to _____.

3. A very small, poor house is a _____.

4. A private high school may be called a _____.

5. To go to a school is to _____ it.

6. The part of yourself that thinks and feels is your _____.

7. To leave is to _____.

8. To be very good at something is to be _____.

9. Someone who has finished school has _____.

10. To believe that good things are possible is to have _____.

Golda Meir

Four-year-old Golda Mabovitz sat on the stairs of her family's home in Kiev, Russia. She watched her father rushing to board up the windows and doors. Golda didn't understand exactly what was happening. But she knew her family was in danger. People in Kiev were planning a pogrom, or attack against the Jews. Because Golda's family was Jewish, they might be attacked. Any minute people might break into their home. These people might set the house on fire. They might rob, beat, or even kill Golda's family.

The Jewish Homeland

The pogrom planned for that day in 1902 never took place. For some reason, people lost interest in the attack. Still, Golda never forgot the fear she felt while watching her father board up the windows. "It's not fair," she thought as she grew older. "We're peaceful people. We shouldn't be attacked just because our **beliefs** are different from those of other people."

Many Jews agreed with Golda. They felt Jews would never be safe until they had their own country. Golda and other Jews dreamed of living in Palestine, an area in the Middle East. This was the old Jewish **homeland**. For years the British had ruled Palestine. Many Arabs also lived there. But Golda hoped that someday this land would again belong to the Jews.

In 1921, Golda made a bold move. She decided she and her husband should live in Palestine. They could help **create** a Jewish state there. In Palestine, Golda went to work for the World Zionist Congress and the Jewish Agency for Palestine. She made speeches and went to meetings. She did all she could to make people see that Jews needed their own country.

American soldiers guard a street in Haifa, Palestine in 1946

During these years, Golda also **struggled** to raise a family. She had little money. Sometimes she took in washing. Often she could hardly afford to feed her children. Still, she had no **regrets**. She believed that Jews would never be safe until they had a home of their own.

No Peace in Palestine

In 1946, Golda became the head of the Jewish Agency. That made her the most **powerful** person among Palestine's Jews. The following year, her wish came true. The United Nations agreed to turn Palestine into two countries. One would be an Arab state. The other would be the Jewish state of Israel.

Jews around the world celebrated when they heard the news. Golda, too, was happy. But she was also worried. She knew that Arabs didn't want half of Palestine. They wanted it all. She feared they would go to war to destroy Israel.

Golda did all she could to keep this war from happening. She gave a speech to the people of Palestine, asking them to honor the United Nations' **vote**. She said, "The United Nations have had their say. Let us now live in friendship and peace together."

But there would be no peace in Palestine. On November 29, 1947, fighting broke out. Arabs burned Jewish stores. They attacked Jewish buses. Arabs in neighboring countries got their armies ready to attack. "If we want to keep our country, we will have to fight for it," thought Golda.

Fighting for Israel

Golda knew the Jews had little chance of winning a war. Arab armies had plenty of guns. They had airplanes

Golda Meir talks with President John F. Kennedy.

and tanks. The Jews had no real army. They needed guns. But to buy guns, they needed money.

Golda decided she would try to get the money. Quickly, she flew to the United States. She asked American Jews to help Israel. She said, "You cannot decide whether we should fight or not. We will. You can only decide one thing — whether we shall be **victorious**. I beg of you, don't be too late. The time is now."

American Jews agreed. In just six weeks, Golda raised $50 million. Said one Israeli, "Someday it will be said that there was a Jewish woman who got the money which made the state possible."

The money that Golda raised was used to strengthen the Israeli army. Although it was difficult, this army fought off the Arabs. In 1956, Golda became Israel's **Foreign Minister**. That same year, she changed her last name from Myerson to Meir. In 1969, she became Israel's **Prime Minister**. She held this post for five years. She kept working to help Israel until her death in 1978.

Do You Remember?

■ Read each sentence below. Write **T** if the sentence is true. Write **F** if the sentence is false.

_____ 1. Golda was Jewish.

_____ 2. Golda lived all her life in Palestine.

_____ 3. Many Arabs lived in Palestine.

_____ 4. Golda raised her children in Palestine.

_____ 5. Golda did not think that Jews should have their own country.

_____ 6. The United Nations voted to make Israel a country.

_____ 7. Most Arabs supported Israel.

_____ 8. Arab armies had no guns or planes.

_____ 9. Golda asked American Jews to help Israel.

_____10. Golda became the Prime Minister of Israel.

Express Yourself

■ Pretend you are Golda Meir. You have come to the United States to ask American Jews to help Israel. Write three or four lines telling what you would say to convince them to help.

_____

_____

_____

_____

_____

_____

Exploring Words

■ Use the clues to complete the puzzle. Choose from the words in the box.

Prime Minister

Foreign Minister

victorious

regrets

struggled

create

homeland

beliefs

vote

powerful

Across
1. things you believe
4. leader of a country
5. worked very hard
6. decision made by a group of people
7. place your ancestors came from
8. being the winner
9. make something new

Down
2. leader who deals with other countries
3. feelings of being sorry
4. having power

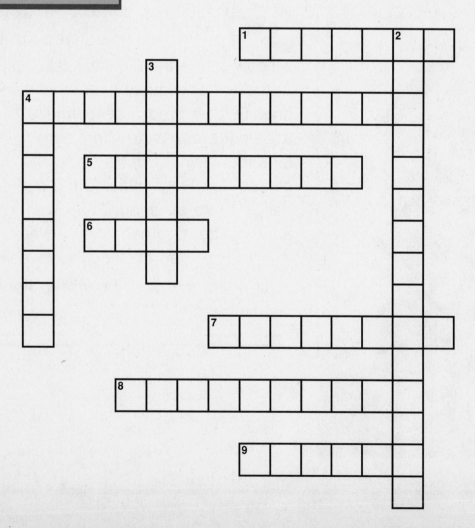

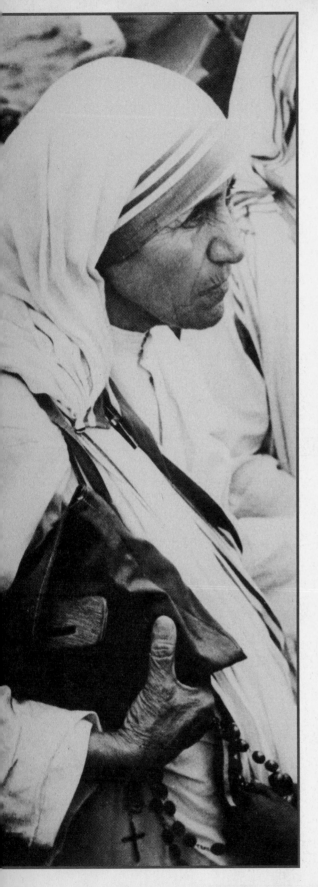

Mother Teresa

Mother Teresa stared out the window of the train in Calcutta, India. Looking at the hot and dusty streets, she felt very uneasy. She lived a peaceful life as a **nun** in a Calcutta **convent** with clean buildings and beautiful lawns. But her quiet life did not please her. Here, outside the convent walls, people were suffering. They lived in doorways and on street corners. Many were sick and dying. They had no food, no love, nothing.

"It isn't right," she thought to herself. "It just isn't right."

Answering a Call

As the train passed through the city, Mother Teresa had a sudden **inspiration**. She felt that God was sending her a message. She later said, "I heard the call to give up all and follow Him into the **slums**, to serve Him in the poorest of the poor. I knew it was His will and that I had to follow Him. The message was quite clear. I was to leave the convent and work with the poor while living among them. It was an order."

On August 16, 1948, Mother Teresa followed this order. She left her convent and went to a hospital in Patna, India. "I need some training," she told the nuns who ran the hospital. "I plan to go out and live among the people. But in order to help them, I must know something about medicine."

Hospital workers were glad to have Mother Teresa's help. At first, she simply held the hand of sick or dying people. Soon, however, she learned to do more. She gave shots and delivered babies. She studied **nutrition**. She learned the uses of different medicines. After three months, she was ready to leave.

Mother Teresa leads a sick man to a home for dying destitutes.

"It is time for me to return to Calcutta," she said. "God's work is waiting for me there."

Living Among the Poor

Back in Calcutta, 38-year-old Mother Teresa went out onto the dirty, crowded streets. She saw a group of children curled up in a doorway. "Come here, children," she called. "We are going to open a school." Right there on the street, Mother Teresa started a school. It had no roof, no walls, no chairs. But that didn't matter.

Word of Mother Teresa's school spread quickly. In February, 1949, a man named Michael Gomes came forward to help. He let Mother Teresa carry on her work on the top floor of his house. She worked with poor children there day after day. Soon other nuns came to help her. Mother Teresa was happy to see them. Still, she warned them that life with her would not be easy.

"You must dress as I dress," she told them. "You must wear a white cotton sari — the dress worn by the poorest of the poor in India. You must live among the dirty, the sick, the blind. You must spend your days helping those who are suffering." By 1949, Mother Teresa had ten nuns working with her. They called themselves the **Missionaries** of **Charity**.

The Greatest Reward

One day Mother Teresa was out walking. She saw an old woman lying in the street. Quickly Mother Teresa ran to help the woman. She scooped her into her arms and rushed her to the hospital. "We cannot take her," the doctors said. "She has no money to pay us."

Mother Teresa was **horrified**. "Cats and dogs are treated better than this," she said. She decided to open her own center for poor people who were sick. She called it the Nirmal Hriday Home for Dying **Destitutes**.

By 1952, people were pouring into this home. Mother Teresa took in babies who had been deserted by their mothers. Some had been found lying in the garbage. She took in lepers, people with ugly sores all over their bodies. Many were blind or crippled. Some were too weak to walk or talk. Mother Teresa fed them all. She gave them medicine. She smiled as some grew stronger. She offered comfort to those who were dying.

As time passed, more and more people noticed what Mother Teresa was doing. Some sent money to help her. Others came to work with her. By 1973, branches of the Missionaries of Charity had opened in 35 Indian cities and a dozen other countries. By 1990, there were 400 branches.

Over the years, Mother Teresa received many **awards** for her work. She won the Pope John XXIII Peace Prize in 1971. She won the Nobel Peace Prize in 1979. For her, however, the greatest reward did not come from prizes. It came from helping those who were most in need.

Mother Teresa visits children at one of her orphans' homes.

Do You Remember?

■ In the blank, write the letter of the best ending for each sentence.

_____ 1. Mother Teresa wanted to help
   a. poor people.   b. her parents.   c. teachers.

_____ 2. Mother Teresa left her convent and went to a
   a. school.   b. hotel.   c. hospital.

_____ 3. Mother Teresa started a
   a. singing group.   b. school.   c. church.

_____ 4. Mother Teresa wore
   a. a purple robe.
   b. fancy clothes.
   c. the same clothes that poor people wore.

_____ 5. Doctors only helped people who had
   a. money.   b. children.   c. important jobs.

_____ 6. Mother Teresa opened a home for
   a. artists.   b. poor, sick people.   c. nurses.

_____ 7. By 1990, the Missionaries of Charity had grown to
   a. 2 branches.   b. 10 branches.   c. 400 branches.

_____ 8. Mother Teresa's greatest reward was
   a. the Nobel Peace Prize.
   b. helping those who were most in need.
   c. making money.

Critical Thinking – Main Ideas

■ Underline the two most important ideas from the story.

1. Mother Teresa was not happy with the quiet life of the convent.

2. Mother Teresa went to a hospital to learn about medicine.

3. Mother Teresa served the poorest of the poor.

4. Michael Gomes let Mother Teresa use the top floor of his house.

5. Mother Teresa started the Missionaries of Charity.

Exploring Words

■ Use the words in the box to complete the paragraphs. Reread the paragraphs to be sure they make sense.

Missionaries	Charity	nun	inspiration	horrified
Destitutes	awards	slums	convent	nutrition

Mother Teresa was a **(1)** _____ who lived in a

(2) _____ in India. One day, while on a train, she had a

sudden **(3)** _____. She believed God was telling her to go live

in the **(4)** _____. There she could help the poor and the sick.

She could give them food, medicine, and love.

Mother Teresa went to a hospital to learn about medicine and

(5) _____. Then she went to Calcutta to live among the

poor. Soon other women joined her. They called themselves the

(6) _____ of **(7)** _____.

One day Mother Teresa took a dying woman to a hospital. She was

(8) _____ to learn that the doctors would only care for the

woman if she had money to pay them. Mother Teresa decided to open

her own home for sick people. Her home, called the Nirmal Hriday Home

for Dying **(9)** _____, cared for those who had no money.

Because of her work among the poor, Mother Teresa won many

(10) _____.

57

Doctor for the Poor

It was 1954, and Tom Dooley was a young Navy doctor from America. He was standing in a camp in Vietnam for **refugees** from the French Indochina War. The camp was crowded with sick, hungry people. They had diseases that had been wiped out long ago in most parts of the world. Almost all were tired and dirty and poor.

Dooley stayed in the camp for several months. He gave the refugees medicine. He bandaged their cuts. Most important, he showed them kindness.

Dooley had cared for many sick people. But he had never seen this much suffering before. He later wrote, "I saw more sickness in a month than most doctors see in a lifetime."

A Country in Need

By the time he left the Navy in 1955, Dooley knew he could not be happy living in the United States again. The U.S. didn't really need another doctor. But in Southeast Asia, doctors were **desperately** needed. There he could do the most good. There he could save the most lives. Dooley decided to go to Laos, the country just west of Vietnam. He wanted to set up a small hospital there.

Dooley knew Laos was a poor country. Still, life there came as a **shock** to him. Laos was even poorer than Vietnam. There was just one real doctor in the whole country. Many of the two million Laotians used **witch doctors**. Many more got no help at all.

In 1956, Dooley opened his hospital in the village of Vang Vieng. Three other Americans helped him. Norman Baker, Peter Kessey, and Dennis Shepard had worked with Dooley at the refugee camp in Vietnam. They admired him very much. Baker and Shepard were both newly married. They didn't want to leave their wives. Still, when Dooley asked them, they came to Laos to help start the hospital.

A Girl Named Savong

Word of Dooley's hospital spread quickly. Every morning Laotians lined up for sick call. They had no money. So they carried chickens, eggs, and vegetables to give to Dooley. These people had every kind of sickness. Dooley could cure some of them. Other people were beyond help. All Dooley could do for them was to make them feel more comfortable.

In the afternoons, Dooley went out on jeep call. He took his jeep to nearby villages and honked his horn. He then opened the back of the jeep. The jeep served as his office. The sick would crawl out of their huts to get help from him.

It was hard work. Dooley saw many people die because they didn't get medicine in time. Sometimes Dooley would wonder if he was doing any good. Then he would glance up at the picture of a 14-year-old girl named Savong. He would remember the good he was doing. The picture of Savong kept Dooley in Laos.

Dooley first met Savong in 1956. An American man was driving along a jungle trail. Suddenly, some Laotians stopped his jeep. They knew a girl who needed help badly. They took the American to Savong, who was lying on the ground, almost dead. He put the girl in his jeep and rushed her to Dooley.

Savong's leg had been badly scratched. No one had cleaned the wound. Dirt got into it. Soon an **infection** developed. As it spread, Savong grew sicker and sicker.

Dooley had seen many poor, dying children in Asia. Many of them were beyond help, but he thought Savong had a chance. So he went to work. After many hours in **surgery**, he had done all he could. The rest was up to Savong.

Then Dooley, Baker, Kessey, and Shepard took turns watching over the girl. Slowly, she began to feel better. One day she smiled. Then she began to cry. She couldn't believe she was still alive. Finally, after several months, she became strong and well. Savong returned to her village. Her picture stayed on Dooley's wall.

Moving to the Mountains

In January, 1957, Dooley left Vang Vieng. He turned the hospital over to Laotians he had trained. Dooley wanted to open a new hospital in Nam Tha, a village high in the mountains. Nam Tha was poorer than Vang Vieng. It had no roads. Supplies had to be brought in by plane or carried in on foot. Dooley's hospital was nothing more than a simple bamboo hut.

Dooley didn't worry about such things. He had too many sick people to think about. He treated dozens of people every day. Some came to the hospital. Many others were too sick to travel. So Dooley often packed up his bag and traveled to the villages. Many times, he had to walk an hour or more to reach them. He had to climb steep rocks and cross rope bridges. At the end of each day, he was **exhausted**. But he was happy to see how much he was helping the people of Nam Tha.

One of the hardest parts of his job was dealing with the people Dooley called witch doctors. As Dooley wrote, "These doctors use sticks, nuts, boiled leaves, and pig grease. Most of their ideas are **fantastic**." These witch doctors often made a sick person even sicker. They rubbed pig grease into cuts. They covered burns with dirt.

Dooley knew they should not do this. Still, he did not want to anger the witch doctors. He knew the Laotians trusted them. He began to work with them. He tried to

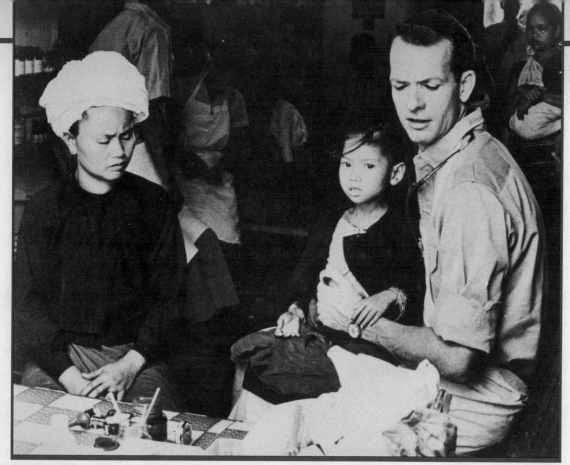
Dooly treats a young girl at his hospital in Vang Vieng.

show them how important it was to wash their hands
and keep cuts clean. In time, he helped them learn a
few rules of modern medicine.

After three years in Southeast Asia, Dooley's own
health began to fail. He went to New York for help. The
doctors found he had **cancer**. He didn't have long to live.
But he wanted to spend what time he had left in Laos.
"I'm not going to quit," he said. "I will continue to guide
and lead my hospitals until my back, my brain, my blood,
and my bones **collapse**."

Dooley did go back to Laos. For a while he was able
to continue his work. But by December, 1960, he was
very sick. He returned to a New York hospital. There, on
January 18, 1961, he died. His life had been short. But
he had done much to help the people of Southeast Asia.

Do You Remember?

■ Read each sentence below. Write **T** if the sentence is true. Write **F** if the sentence is false.

_____ 1. Tom Dooley was a pilot in the United States Air Force.

_____ 2. Laos was a poor country.

_____ 3. Dooley went to Laos because he couldn't find work in the United States.

_____ 4. Dooley saved Savong's life.

_____ 5. Laotians often paid Dooley with eggs and vegetables instead of money.

_____ 6. Dooley's hospital in Nam Tha was a large, new building.

_____ 7. Dooley did not allow Laotians to work in his hospitals.

_____ 8. Dooley died of cancer.

Express Yourself

■ Pretend you are a reporter who has been sent to interview Tom Dooley at his hospital in Nam Tha. What questions would you ask Dr. Dooley?

_____

_____

_____

_____

_____

_____

_____

Exploring Words

■ Use the words in the box to complete the paragraphs. Reread the paragraphs to be sure they make sense.

| infection | surgery | refugees | witch doctors | shock |
| fantastic | collapse | exhausted | desperately | cancer |

Tom Dooley worked in Vietnam in a camp for **(1)** _____.

Later he moved to Laos and opened his own hospital. It was a

(2) _____ for him to see what a poor country Laos was.

They **(3)** _____ needed his help. Every day he worked until

he was **(4)** _____. He saved many lives. He saved the life

of a girl with a bad **(5)** _____ in her leg by performing

(6) _____ on her.

Dooley also worked with Laotian **(7)** _____. These people

had **(8)** _____ ideas about how to help the sick. Dooley was

able to teach the witch doctors some rules of modern medicine.

After three years in Laos, Dooley learned he had **(9)** _____.

Still, he continued to work. He said he would keep helping Laotians until

his **(10)** _____.

Martin Luther King, Jr.

Martin Luther King, Jr., walked into a restaurant in Atlanta, Georgia. He and a friend wanted to have lunch together.

"We'd like a table for two," said King.

The woman looked at King, who was black. She looked at his friend, who was white. Then she shook her head. "I'll have to seat you at a **separate** table," she told King. She pointed to a table on the other side of a curtain. That was the only place in the **restaurant** where blacks could eat.

Fighting for Freedom

Dr. King was not surprised. In 1960, blacks all across America were treated differently from whites. Blacks were not allowed to sit at white lunch **counters** or swim at white beaches. They were not allowed to use white bathrooms or attend white churches. This separation of blacks from whites was called segregation. As long as there was segregation, blacks would not have many rights.

Dr. King knew that segregation was wrong. As a **minister** in the Baptist Church, he believed that all people were the children of God. The color of a person's skin did not matter.

In 1955, Dr. King became a leader in the fight to end segregation. He helped carry out a bus **boycott** in Montgomery, Alabama. Before the boycott, blacks could sit only in the back of buses. Then, on December 5, 1955, blacks stopped riding the buses. They refused to ride until all seats were opened to them.

The boycott lasted one year. For Dr. King, it was a difficult and sometimes scary year. Some whites were

Dr. King leads a march from Selma, Alabama to Montgomery, Alabama in 1965.

very angry about the boycott. They tried to frighten blacks into giving up. One night while Dr. King was away giving a speech, whites **bombed** his home. King rushed home to make sure his wife and baby daughter were all right. Luckily, they had not been hurt. But King knew that next time they might not be so lucky.

Meeting Hate with Love

Many blacks wanted to get even for the bombing. But Dr. King was a peaceful man. He did not believe in violence. He spoke to the blacks who gathered outside his home after the bombing. "Go home and put down your weapons," he said. "We cannot solve problems with **violence**. We must learn to meet hate with love."

Finally, after a year, the boycott worked. The city of Montgomery allowed blacks to sit in any seat they chose. Dr. King was pleased. But he knew there were many other battles to fight. There were still many laws that segregated blacks. King wanted these laws changed. He wanted America to be a land of freedom for all people.

Blacks could now ride buses with whites. But they still could not eat at most restaurants and lunch counters. If a black person wanted to eat at a restaurant, he had to go to the back door. When he paid, the food was handed out.

Students in the South didn't think this was right. They knew of Dr. King's teachings. They had read about the bus boycott. These students decided to hold sit-ins in restaurants and lunch counters all over the South.

Together black and white students would enter restaurants and ask to be served. They went into stores and sat down at lunch counters. Angry white people poured sugar, salt, and coffee over the students' heads. But the students would not leave until they had been served. Sometimes the students were arrested and taken to jail.

Dr. King is arrested at a lunch counter.

In 1960, students asked Dr. King to join them in a sit-in at a large lunch counter in Atlanta, Georgia. When they sat down and asked to be served, Dr. King and the students were arrested. Dr. King was not ashamed to go to jail. He believed there was honor in standing up for his beliefs. He said, "I'll stay in jail one year or ten years if it takes that long to stop segregation in these stores."

After a few days, Dr. King was freed. Over the next several years, police arrested him many times. Each time he went peacefully. He knew in his heart that he was fighting for what was right.

A Dream for America

By 1963, King was the most famous black man in the country. His words and actions were helping people see that segregation was wrong. On August 28, 1963, blacks held a march on Washington. Two hundred and fifty thousand people came, both black and white, to show their support. There Dr. King gave his best-known speech.

"I have a dream," he told the crowd. "I have a dream that one day on the red hills of Georgia the sons of former **slaves** and the sons of former slaveowners will be able to sit down together at the table of brotherhood."

He said, "I have a dream that my four little children one day will live in a nation where they will not be judged by the color of their skin but by the **content** of their **character**."

"This is our hope," said King. "This is the faith that I go back to the South with. With this faith we will be able to work together, to pray together, to go to jail together, to stand up for freedom together, knowing that we will be free one day."

"This will be the day," King said, "when all of God's children will be able to sing with new meaning, "Let freedom ring.""

"And when we allow freedom to ring," he said, "when we let it ring from every village, from every state and every city, we will be able to speed up that day when all God's children, black men and white men, will be able to join hands and sing, "Free at last! Free at last! Thank God Almighty, we are free at last!"

For the next five years, Dr. Martin Luther King, Jr., kept fighting to end segregation. He led many peaceful marches and gatherings. He worked with world leaders and spoke to millions of people. Dr. King and his followers won many battles. They got many laws changed.

On April 4, 1968, Dr. King's life was cut short. A white man named James Earl Ray shot and killed Dr. King in Memphis, Tennessee. People all over the country were shocked. They couldn't believe that such a great leader was gone. Although Dr. King did not live to see his dream come true, he helped end segregation in America. For that, he will always be a national hero.

Do You Remember?

■ In the blank, write the letter of the best ending for each sentence.

_____ 1. Dr. Martin Luther King, Jr. wanted to
     a. win rights for blacks.
     b. bomb white churches.
     c. move to Africa.

_____ 2. Dr. King was often
     a. arrested.   b. wrong.   c. late to work.

_____ 3. Dr. King believed that the color of a person's skin
     a. was very important.
     b. didn't matter.
     c. was more important than his or her character.

_____ 4. In his most famous speech, Dr. King said,
     a. "Black is beautiful."
     b. "I have a dream."
     c. "Whites should have fewer rights than blacks."

Critical Thinking – Cause and Effect

■ Complete the following sentences.

1. Dr. King could not eat with his white friend in the Atlanta restaurant

because _____

2. Blacks in Montgomery stopped riding the city buses because _____

_____

3. Dr. King told the blacks who had gathered outside his house after the

bombing to go home because _____

4. Dr. King was not ashamed to go to jail because _____

_____

Exploring Words

■ Write the correct word in each sentence.

separate	counters	boycott	violence	content
restaurant	minister	bombed	slaves	character

1. Something that is kept apart from something else is _____.

2. People who are owned by someone else are _____.

3. A _____ is the head of a church.

4. If you _____ something, you made it explode.

5. A business that serves food is a _____.

6. To refuse to do business with a company is to _____ that company.

7. What a person believes and how that person behaves is his or her _____.

8. The _____ of something is what it is made up of.

9. Flat surfaces where food is served are _____.

10. If you use force to harm someone, you use _____.

Beating the Odds

Five-year-old Evonne Goolagong sat on the steps of her parents' house in Barellan, Australia. She watched some older children batting a tennis ball around. "When will I be able to play tennis?" she asked her mother.

"Evonne," said her mother sadly, "you know we don't have money for things like tennis rackets."

Evonne knew her mother was right. The Goolagongs were very poor. Evonne's father worked **shearing** sheep. He didn't make much money. Sometimes he couldn't even afford to feed his eight children. Evonne knew he could never afford to buy her a tennis racket. Still, she kept dreaming of tennis. To her, it seemed like the most wonderful game in the world.

A Special Gift

One day Evonne picked up an old broomstick and a tennis ball. "Look, Mum!" she cried happily. "This broomstick can be my tennis racket!"

For the next few months, Evonne practiced with the broomstick. Then an aunt found out how much Evonne loved tennis. The aunt gave her a racket as a present. Evonne was thrilled. "I used to sleep with that racket," she later said. She played with it every chance she got.

Evonne played at the Barellan War **Memorial** Tennis Club. It had a dusty dirt court with a **sagging** net. Hour after hour Evonne played there. Bill Kurtzmann, the club president, noticed how good she was. He started to help her with her tennis. In 1961, he entered 10-year-old Evonne in a small **tournament**. It turned out that the tournament was for women, not girls. Evonne didn't care. She decided to play against the women. She won easily.

Clearly Evonne had a special **talent**. But what could she do with it? She was a poor Aborigine. Aborigines are black Australians. Their history is much like that of the **Native** Americans. The Aborigines settled in Australia long before white people. But whites later drove them off the land. Most ended up in **barren** parts of Australia. As a result, most Aborigines are poor, with little hope for the **future**.

Like many other Aborigines, Evonne seemed trapped by her family's **poverty**. Talent scouts came to watch her. They could see she had real talent. But without good training, she could not become a top player. And the Goolagongs couldn't afford good training.

Following Her Dream

In 1961, Vic Edwards heard about Evonne. Edwards was the best tennis teacher in Australia. He invited Evonne to spend a few weeks at his club in Sydney. But the Goolagongs couldn't afford to send her. "I'm sorry, Evonne," said her father. "We just don't have the money."

The Goolagongs' friends and neighbors wanted to help Evonne. They could see she was special. They believed in her and her talent. Quickly they raised money. They bought Evonne new clothes and a plane ticket. They sent her off to Edwards' club in Sydney.

With Edwards' help, Evonne became better and better. When she was 14 years old, Edwards went to see her parents. He asked if Evonne could come live with his family year round. "That way she could have the training she needs," he said.

The Goolagongs agreed. They wanted to give Evonne the chance to follow her dream. From then on, Edwards worked with Evonne every day. He helped her with her tennis game. He also made sure she studied hard and finished high school.

Beating the Best

By the time she was 19 years old, Evonne was a big name in the world of tennis. Between 1968 and 1970, she won 44 tournaments in Australia. In 1971, she won the French Open. Her friends and family back in Barellan cheered each time they heard of a Goolagong victory. "Soon she'll be the best in the world," they said to each other.

Vic Edwards was thinking the same thing. In August of 1971, he entered Evonne in England's Wimbledon tournament. This was the most important tournament in the world. "Good luck," he said to her as Wimbledon began. "And remember — you're not really alone out there. There are a lot of people who believe in you."

Evonne easily won the early rounds. In the final match, she faced Margaret Court. Court was a white Australian. She was the best woman tennis player in the world. Could Evonne beat her?

On the day of the big match, Evonne played brilliantly. She beat Court by winning two straight **sets**. This was only the beginning. Goolagong continued to win tournaments throughout the 1970's. She showed that money and skin color are not important. She proved that with talent, hard work, and good friends, anything is possible.

Do You Remember?

■ Read each sentence below. Write **T** if the sentence is true. Write **F** if the sentence is false.

_____ 1. Evonne Goolagong came from a rich family.

_____ 2. For several months, Evonne used a broomstick as a tennis racket.

_____ 3. Evonne's aunt took away Evonne's tennis racket.

_____ 4. Vic Edwards didn't think Evonne had talent.

_____ 5. Evonne's neighbors raised money so Evonne could get good training.

_____ 6. Evonne's parents refused to let her play tennis.

_____ 7. Evonne never beat Margaret Court.

_____ 8. In 1971, Evonne won the Wimbledon tennis tournament.

Express Yourself

■ Pretend you are one of Evonne Goolagong's parents. Would you let Evonne live with Vic Edwards' family? Why or why not?

_____

_____

_____

_____

_____

_____

_____

Exploring Words

■ Read each sentence. Fill in the circle next to the best meaning for the word in dark print. You may use a dictionary.

1. Evonne's father worked **shearing** sheep.
   ○ a. moving   ○ b. cutting wool off   ○ c. killing

2. Evonne played at the Barellan War **Memorial** Tennis club.
   ○ a. in honor of   ○ b. for members only   ○ c. indoor

3. The club had a dusty dirt court with a **sagging** net.
   ○ a. huge   ○ b. new   ○ c. falling down

4. Vic entered Evonne in a small **tournament**.
   ○ a. contest   ○ b. book   ○ c. journey

5. Clearly Evonne had a special **talent**.
   ○ a. language   ○ b. skill   ○ c. job

6. The Aborigines' history is much like that of **Native** Americans.
   ○ a. enemies of   ○ b. born in a place   ○ c. angry

7. They ended up in the most **barren** parts of Australia.
   ○ a. where things don't grow
   ○ b. filled with people
   ○ c. beautiful

8. Most Aborigines had little hope for the **future**.
   ○ a. yesterday   ○ b. the time yet to come   ○ c. today

9. Evonne seemed trapped by her family's **poverty**.
   ○ a. orders   ○ b. money   ○ c. having no money

10. She beat Court by winning two straight **sets**.
   ○ a. groups of games   ○ b. bets   ○ c. chairs

The Fight for Peace

Archbishop Oscar Romero sat back in his chair. It had been another hard day. Romero had given a speech, visited the poor, and buried a friend. He just wanted to close his eyes and rest.

Then he noticed a letter on his desk. Putting on his glasses, he opened the envelope and read the note. It said, "Stick to church business or else!"

The note was not signed. There was just a rough drawing of a human **skull**.

"Another death threat," said Romero softly. "Someday the threat will be real."

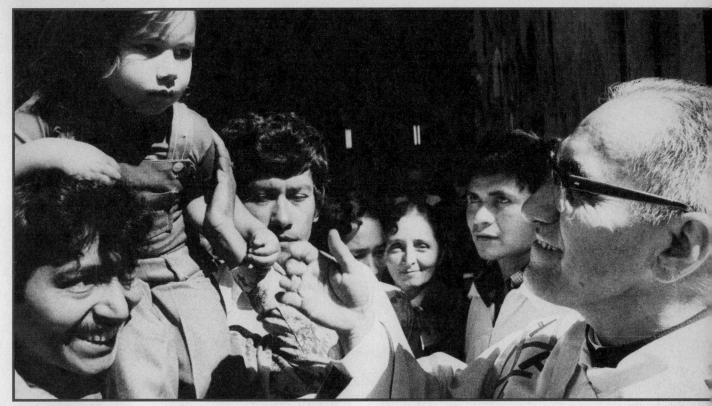

Archbishop Romero visits with members of his church.

A Friend is Killed

Oscar Romero became the archbishop of San Salvador in 1977. San Salvador is the capital of El Salvador, a country in Central America. At first, people didn't know what Romero would do. As a Catholic **priest**, he had been very quiet. He had done his work for the Catholic church. But that was it. He had not been interested in **politics**. He had not said anything about the hard times faced by his country's poor people. He had believed that his only job in life was to serve the church.

As archbishop, however, all of this changed. Romero began speaking out about other things. He called attention to the suffering of the poor. He asked the government to help its people. When the government refused, he spoke out against the country's leaders. What caused this change in Romero? What made him enter the world of politics?

The change came after the death of his old friend, Rutilio Grande. Grande was a priest in the village of Aguilares. He worked closely with the poor people there. Grande tried to get them better pay. They earned just $3 a day cutting sugar cane under the hot sun. Rich **landowners** did not like Grande, and neither did government leaders. They all wanted him to mind his own business. On March 12, 1977, someone shot and killed this gentle priest.

Romero was very upset about his friend's death. He asked the government to find the killer. The government did nothing. Instead, it sent soldiers into Aguilares. The government said these soldiers were going to keep the peace. But instead, they began fighting the villagers. They killed fifty people and beat others. They dragged some off to prison. Soldiers also broke into the church. They blasted it with bullets.

Romero went to the church and tried to clean it up. The soldiers stopped him. That was when he knew he had to speak out. His days as a quiet priest were over.

Working for the Poor

Things did not get better. Over the next three years, the government's actions did not change.

Government leaders still worked only to help the rich. And armed men continued to kill people. Six more priests were killed. Others were taken away in the middle of the night and beaten. Many poor people simply disappeared. Others were killed in the middle of the day by **death squads**.

Romero did what he could to change things. He begged the government to stop the killings. Every Sunday in church he read the names of the people who had been killed during the week. Poor people came to Romero with pictures of family members who

People visit the tomb of Archbishop Oscar Romero.

had disappeared. He was able to free some. Others he found dead. Still others were never seen again.

Outside of El Salvador, Romero was thought of as a hero. He was **nominated** for a Nobel Peace Prize in 1979. Inside El Salvador, however, rich landowners were becoming more and more unhappy with him. In February, 1980, someone tried to blow up his church.

The Death of a Hero

Romero knew his life was in danger. But he refused to be silent. During a church service on March 23, 1980, he spoke directly to the army and the government. "I beg you, I order you, to stop the **repression**."

The next night he went to a hospital and held a church service for sick people. During the service, Romero spoke about the need for peace. Suddenly, a shot rang out. The bullet struck Romero in the heart. As he lay dying, he whispered, "May God have **mercy** on the **assassins**."

Romero's killer was never found. Many people think El Salvador's leaders played a part in the shooting. Although Romero is dead, his memory lives on, giving hope and strength to the poor people of El Salvador.

Do You Remember?

■ In the blank, write the letter of the best ending for each sentence.

_____ 1. Oscar Romero was a member of the
   a. Baptist Church.   b. government.   c. Catholic church.

_____ 2. Rutilio Grande was
   a. a priest.   b. a rich man.   c. Romero's father.

_____ 3. In Aguilares, government soldiers
   a. cleaned up the church.
   b. destroyed the church.
   c. asked Romero for help.

_____ 4. Romero tried to help
   a. the poor people of El Salvador.
   b. government soldiers.
   c. American farmers.

_____ 5. People outside of El Salvador thought Romero was
   a. crazy.   b. a hero.   c. mean.

Critical Thinking – Fact or Opinion?

■ Write **F** before each statement that is a fact. Write **O** before each statement that is an opinion.

_____ 1. Oscar Romero was the bravest man in El Salvador.

_____ 2. Romero was foolish to speak out against the government.

_____ 3. Romero received angry notes and death threats.

_____ 4. Romero tried to help the poor people of his country.

_____ 5. Romero should have been more careful.

_____ 6. Romero knew his life was in danger.

_____ 7. Romero should have won the Nobel Peace Prize.

_____ 8. Romero was killed during a church service at a hospital.

Exploring Words

■ Use the clues to complete the puzzle. Choose from the words in the box.

skull

priest

politics

landowners

death squads

nominated

archbishop

repression

assassins

mercy

Across
2. Rutilio Grande was one
4. the work of government
6. killers
8. head bone
9. suggested for an honor or position
10. high church officer

Down
1. being kind
3. allowing no freedom
5. people who own land
7. groups of soldiers who kill enemies of the government

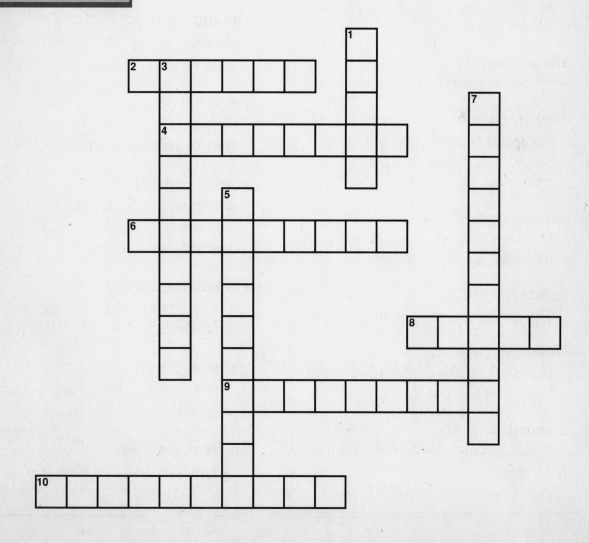

Glossary

acid, page 24
Acid is a chemical that can burn your skin.

angel, page 4
Christians believe that an angel is a messenger of God.

archbishop, page 80
An archbishop is an important church leader.

armor, page 5
Armor is metal clothing worn long ago to protect the body in battles.

assassins, page 83
Assassins are people who kill well-known persons.

attend, page 40
To attend means to go to.

awards, page 55
An award is something given to someone to honor that person for something she or he has done.

barren, page 76
A barren place is one that is dry and has few plants or animals.

beliefs, page 47
The things you believe are your beliefs.

bloodiest, page 18
Bloodiest means causing the greatest harm to many people.

bombed, page 69
If you bombed something, you made it explode.

boycott, page 68
To boycott a company is to refuse to do business with that company.

cancer, page 63
Cancer is a sickness that spreads through a person's body.

capital, page 18
The capital of a country is the seat of its government.

character, page 70
A person's character is what she or he thinks and believes, and how she or he behaves.

Charity, page 54
To give charity is to offer help to those who need it.

collapse, page 63
To collapse is to fall down or reach the end of your strength.

colors, page 12
When you show a flag that tells who you are, it is sometimes called showing your colors.

confidence, page 7
If you have confidence, you feel sure of yourself.

content, page 70
The content of something is what is inside it or what it is made up of.

convent, page 52
A convent is where nuns live.

counters, page 68
Counters in a restaurant are long, flat surfaces where people can eat.

courage, page 7
To have courage is to be brave.

create, page 47
To create means to make something that wasn't there before.

crouching, page 24
If you are crouching, your body is bent down close to the ground.

death, page 35
Death is the end of life.

death squads, page 82
Death squads are groups of soldiers whose job it is to kill people who are enemies of the government.

defeat, page 19
Defeat is the act of losing.

demanded, page 12
If you demanded something, you asked for it as though it was your right.

Depart, page 43
To depart means to leave.

desperately, page 60
Desperately means very badly or very much.

Destitutes, page 54
If you are destitute, you are without a home or money.

disease, page 24
To have a disease is to be sick.

dump, page 43
A dump is a place where people take their garbage.

educate, page 43
To educate means to teach.

exhausted, page 62
Exhausted means very tired.

Faith, page 43
To have faith means to believe that good things are possible.

fantastic, page 62
Something fantastic is something amazing or made up.

fled, page 18
If you fled something, you ran away from it.

Foreign Minister, page 49
A foreign minister is a person in the government who meets with the leaders of other countries.

foreigners, page 18
Foreigners are people from another country.

future, page 76
The future is the time yet to come.

governor, page 11
A governor in the United States is a leader in charge of a state.

graduated, page 41
If you graduated, you finished school.

hired, page 24
If you hired someone, you gave that person a job.

homeland, page 47

Your homeland is the place where you were born, or the place your ancestors came from.

honorable, page 31

To be honorable means to have honor.

horrified, page 54

To be horrified means to be surprised in a way that is not pleasant.

horror, page 23

Horror is a feeling of fear.

infection, page 61

An infection is a sickness in the body.

injured, page 34

To be injured means to be hurt.

Inspector, page 25

An inspector is a person in charge of checking to see that rules are being followed.

inspiration, page 53

An inspiration is an idea or a belief that comes to you suddenly.

inspire, page 7

If something inspires you, it makes you feel full of hope.

invaded, page 16

Invaded means entered by force.

labor, page 25

Labor is work.

landowners, page 82

Landowners are people who own land.

liberty, page 19

Liberty is freedom.

lieutenant, page 12

A lieutenant is an officer in the Army or Navy.

loyal, page 17

To be loyal is to be true to someone or something.

Memorial, page 75

A memorial is something built to remind people of someone or something.

memory, page 7

A memory is something remembered. The memory of someone dead is what you remember about that person.

mercy, page 83

To show mercy means to be kind to your enemies.

minister, page 68

A minister is a leader of a Protestant church.

Missionaries, page 54

Missionaries are people sent by a church to help people in other countries.

Native, page 76

A native is someone born in a place. Native Americans are the people who lived in America before the white settlers arrived.

neared, page 32

If you neared something, you came near to it.

noble, page 35

A noble person is brave and kind, and has honor.

nominated, page 83
If you have been nominated for an honor, you may be chosen to receive that honor.

nun, page 52
A nun is a woman of the church who has promised to spend her life helping others.

nutrition, page 53
The study of nutrition is the study of the way the human body uses food.

outstanding, page 41
To be outstanding means to be very good.

pirate, page 10
A pirate is a person who robs ships at sea.

politics, page 81
Politics is the work of government.

poverty, page 76
If you live in poverty, you are very poor.

powerful, page 48
Someone who is powerful has power.

priest, page 81
A priest is a man of the church.

Prime Minister, page 49
A prime minister is the leader of a country. Prime ministers are much like our president.

quarter, page 12
To give quarter in a battle means to fight only until you have won, and not kill every one of your enemy.

refugees, page 59
A refugee is a person who leaves his country because of war.

regrets, page 48
To have regrets means to wish that you had done things differently.

rejoiced, page 13
If you rejoiced, you were glad about something.

repression, page 83
Repression means holding something down or controlling it by force.

restaurant, page 67
A restaurant is a business that serves food.

rude, page 26
To be rude to someone means to behave badly toward that person.

sagging, page 75
When something is sagging it is falling down.

saints, page 4
A saint is a person who spent her or his life doing God's work, and who has been honored by a church.

Seminary, page 41
A seminary is a private high school.

separate, page 67
If something is separate, it is kept apart from something else.

sets, page 77
In tennis, a set is a group of games.

settlement, page 32
A settlement is a town of settlers.

settlers, page 31
Settlers are people who move to a
new place.

shack, page 40
A shack is a very small, poor house.

shearing, page 74
If you are shearing a sheep, you are
clipping its wool.

shock, page 60
A shock is a surprise that is
not pleasant.

skull, page 80
Your skull is made up of the bones in
your head and face.

slaves, page 70
If you are a slave, you are owned by
someone and forced to obey and work
for that person.

slums, page 53
Slums are very poor neighborhoods.

soul, page 41
Your soul is the part of yourself that
thinks and feels.

spared, page 10
To be spared means not to be harmed.

struggled, page 48
If you struggled, you worked very hard.

surgery, page 61
When a doctor does surgery, he or
she fixes things inside the body.

surrender, page 6
To surrender is to give up.

suspiciously, page 3
If you looked at someone suspiciously,
you looked at that person as though
you didn't trust her or him.

talent, page 76
If you have a talent, you are able to do
something well.

terrified, page 10
Terrified means filled with terror.

threats, page 26
Threats are promises to cause harm.

tide, page 13
The tide is the rising and falling of
the oceans.

Toiling, page 25
Toiling means working hard.

tournament, page 75
A tournament is a championship series
of games.

treated, page 32
The way you treated someone is the
way you behaved toward that person.

tyrants, page 19
Tyrants are cruel leaders.

uniforms, page 18
Uniforms are clothes that all look the
same, and are worn by a group of
people.

urged, page 35
If you urged someone to do something,
you tried your hardest to get that person
to do it.

victorious, page 49
If you are victorious, you are the winner.

victory, page 5

Victory is success.

violence, page 69

If you used violence, you used force to harm someone.

vote, page 48

A vote is a decision.

welcomed, page 31

If you welcomed someone, you made that person feel at home.

witch doctors, page 60

Witch doctors are medicine men or women who use plants, prayer, and other things to help people who are sick.

Chart Your Progress

Stories	Do You Remember?	Exploring Words	Critical Thinking	Express Yourself	Score
Joan of Arc					/23
A Pirate's Last Stand					/22
Fighting for Freedom					/23
The Voice of the Children					/19
Chief Joseph					/23
Teacher with a Dream					/25
Golda Meir					/25
Mother Teresa					/23
Doctor for the Poor					/23
Martin Luther King, Jr.					/18
Beating the Odds					/23
The Fight for Peace					/23

Finding Your Score
1. Count the number of correct answers you have for each activity.
2. Write these numbers in the boxes in the chart.
3. Ask your teacher to give you a score (maximum score 5) for **Express Yourself**.
4. Add up the numbers to get a final score.

Answer Key

Joan of Arc
Pages 2-9

Do You Remember? 1-F, 2-T, 3-F, 4-T, 5-T, 6-F, 7-T, 8-F

Express Yourself: Answers will vary.

Exploring Words: 1. angel, 2. saints, 3. suspiciously, 4. armor, 5. confidence, 6. victory, 7. surrender, 8. memory, 9. courage, 10. inspire

A Pirate's Last Stand
Pages 10-15

Do You Remember? 1-b, 2-a, 3-a, 4-c, 5-b, 6-b, 7-c

Critical Thinking — Finding the Sequence: 3, 5, 1, 2, 4

Exploring Words: 1. pirate, 2. spared, 3. rejoiced, 4. lieutenant, 5. terrified, 6. governor, 7. tide, 8. demanded, 9. quarter, 10. colors

Fighting for Freedom
Pages 16-21

Do You Remember? 1-T, 2-F, 3-T, 4-F, 5-F, 6-T, 7-F, 8-T

Express Yourself: Answers will vary.

Exploring Words: Across: 1. loyal, 4. bloodiest, 6. tyrants, 7. invaded, 9. uniforms

Down: 1. liberty, 2. fled, 3. foreigners, 5. capital, 8. defeat

The Voice of the Children
Pages 22-29

Do You Remember? 1-c, 2-b, 3-a, 4-b,

Critical Thinking — Drawing Conclusions:

Answers may vary.

Here are some examples.

1. many factory owners kept their workroom doors locked and the workers could not escape the fire.

2. she wanted to stop factory owners from using child workers.

3. she took factory owners who would not stop using child workers to court and made them pay fines.

4. she knew that disease could be passed on to people who bought the clothes.

Exploring Words: 1-a, 2-b, 3-c, 4-a, 5-b, 6-c, 7-a, 8-c, 9-c, 10-b

Chief Joseph
Page 30-37

Do You Remember? 1-F, 2-T, 3-F, 4-F, 5-T, 6-T, 7-F, 8-T

Express Yourself: Answers will vary.

Exploring Words: 1. honorable, 2. welcomed, 3. settlers, 4. treated, 5. urged, 6. injured, 7. settlements, 8. neared, 9. death, 10. noble

Teacher with a Dream
Page 38-45

Do You Remember? 1-b, 2-a, 3-c, 4-b, 5-a

Critical Thinking — Fact or Opinion: 1-F, 2-O, 3-O, 4-F, 5-F, 6-O, 7-F, 8-O, 9-O, 10-F

Exploring Words: 1. dump, 2. educate, 3. shack, 4. seminary, 5. attend, 6. soul, 7. depart, 8. outstanding, 9. graduated, 10. faith

Golda Meir
Page 46-51

Do You Remember? 1-T, 2-F, 3-T, 4-T, 5-F, 6-T, 7-F, 8-F, 9-T, 10-T

Express Yourself: Answers will vary.

Exploring Words: Across: 1. beliefs, 4. Prime Minister, 5. struggled, 6. vote, 7. homeland, 8. victorious, 9. create

Down: 2. Foreign Minister, 3. regrets, 4. powerful

Mother Teresa

Pages 52-57

Do You Remember? 1-a, 2-c, 3-b, 4-c, 5-a, 6-b, 7-c, 8-b

Critical Thinking — Main Ideas: 3, 5

Exploring Words: 1. nun, 2. convent, 3. inspiration, 4. slums, 5. nutrition, 6. Missionaries, 7. Charity, 8. horrified, 9. Destitutes, 10. awards

Doctor for the Poor

Pages 58-65

Do You Remember? 1-F, 2-T, 3-F, 4-T, 5-T, 6-F, 7-F, 8-T

Express Yourself: Answers will vary.

Exploring Words: 1. refugees, 2. shock, 3. desperately, 4. exhausted, 5. infection, 6. surgery, 7. witch doctors, 8. fantastic, 9. cancer, 10. collapse

Martin Luther King, Jr.

Pages 66-73

Do You Remember? 1-a, 2-a, 3-b, 4-b

Critical Thinking — Cause and Effect: Answers may vary. Here are some examples.
1. blacks had to eat in their own part of the restaurant.

2. they could sit only in the backs of buses.
3. problems cannot be solved with violence.
4. he felt there was honor in standing up for his beliefs.

Exploring Words: 1. separate, 2. slaves, 3. minister, 4. bombed, 5. restaurant, 6. boycott, 7. character, 8. content, 9. counters, 10. violence

Beating the Odds

Pages 74-79

Do You Remember? 1-F, 2-T, 3-F, 4-F, 5-T, 6-F, 7-F, 8-T

Express Yourself: Answers will vary.

Exploring Words: 1-b, 2-a, 3-c, 4-a, 5-b, 6-b, 7-a, 8-b, 9-c, 10-a

The Fight for Peace

Pages 80-85

Do You Remember? 1-c, 2-a, 3-b, 4-a, 5-b

Critical Thinking — Fact or Opinion? 1-O, 2-O, 3-F, 4-F, 5-O, 6-F, 7-O, 8-F

Exploring Words: Across: 2. priest, 4. politics, 6. assassins, 8. skull, 9. nominated, 10. archbishop
Down: 1. mercy, 3. repression, 5. landowners, 7. death squads